A BOUQUET
from
HEAVEN

*Celebrating God's
Magnificence through His
Gift of Wildflowers*

A BOUQUET *from* HEAVEN

Celebrating God's
Magnificence through His
Gift of Wildflowers

MELVA STEPHENS LARD

Illustrations by
STEVE MCGUIRE

New Leaf Press

First Printing: January 1997

Copyright 1997 by New leaf Press. All rights reserved. Printed in the
United States of America. No part of this book may be used or reproduced
in any manner whatsoever without written permission of the publisher,
except in the case of brief quotations in articles and reviews. For informa-
tion write: New Leaf Press, Inc., P.O. Box 726, Green Forest, AR 72638

ISBN: 0-89221-325-6
Library of Congress Catalog: 96-069681

Unless otherwise noted, all Scripture quotations are from the King James
Version of the Bible.

Cover Design by Left Coast Design, Inc.

Dedications

Lovingly dedicated to my mother, Eula, who shares my love of wildflowers, and loves me as God does — unconditionally!

– Melva Stephens Lard

To my wife, Debby, and my son Weston . . . thank you for all your support.

– Steve McGuire

Acknowlegements

Hugs and sincere thanks to —

Ruth Storvick — my Alaskan friend, upon whom God has bestowed the precious gift of encouragement. So unsure of myself, shaking all the way to my toes, I shared with Ruth my thoughts for this book and read the first two or three pages I had written. Her enthusiastic support gave me courage to complete the manuscript and seek out a publisher. Had she even hinted of a "ho-hum" attitude, this path to completion would have been extremely rocky.

Lisa Holcombe and Doris Woods — my neighbors and proofreaders. Amazing how they caught all those mistakes I so happily read right over.

Wayne Douglas Lard — my son, for the use of his computer, expertise, and patience.

– Melva Stephens Lard

Contents

INTRODUCTION

A blackberry patch is an unlikely place for the birth of a book. Nevertheless, the infant thoughts that grew and multiplied into this book began there the morning I discovered Ruellias (page 46) growing among the briers.

As a life-long lover of wildflowers, retirement to rural northwest Alabama gave me the "campus," and the time, to become a serious student. Searching, pouring over identification books, drawing, and painting the myriad of flowers about my home delights my days from early March until late October.

Unexpectedly, that morning in the brier patch, I added a spiritual dimension to my study of wildflowers. The presence of God was undeniable. The voice of my teacher, the Holy Spirit, was too strong to be ignored or rationalized away as my own thoughts. The spiritual lesson was clear; I was deeply touched.

Following my meeting with Ruellias, I began to see wildflowers with spiritual eyes, seeing in their names, habits or circumstances, lessons about the character of God, the believer's position and walk with Him, and our relationship with other Christians.

As I meditated on the flowers and the lessons they taught, I realized others would be blessed if they could share in my experience. *Write a book* came the thought — quickly followed by . . . *impossible!* How could I, with only a basic thought of spiritual application for each flower, expand that thought into a book? Amazingly, when I sat down to write, the words flowed from my pen effortlessly and quickly — leaving me forever changed in the degree of my faith and walk with God, my belief in His dealings with His people today, and in answered prayer.

Yes, my name is on the front of this book, but it really isn't mine. It is God's book. I am simply the instrument through which He chose to write it. What a picture of Grace! Amazing Grace!

All of these 30 flowers grow about my home. Some of them, however, range as far north as Alaska, west to the Pacific, and east to the Atlantic. Although some species may be called by different names in different locations, the scientific name will always be the same.

If this book sparks an interest in wildflowers or causes you to see flowers where you once saw only weeds, then I am doubly blessed. As you read of God's example of Grace in nature — the wildflowers — may He touch your life as He has touched mine; with renewed awareness that He is all about us if we will only stop our hurrying, see with eyes of the Spirit, and listen to His voice within.

~ *Eight* ~

Every summer, after the green beans are canned, pickles made, potatoes dug, corn, squash, and peas neatly packaged in the freezer, we follow the wild geese to Alaska. Early adventurers to the "Great Land" were lured by gold. We are lured by a more precious treasure — two daughters, two fine sons-in-law, and three grandchildren!

Our pastures are neatly "bush-hogged" before we leave. Somehow, last year, the lower pasture was missed. Upon our return, we were dazzled with a golden sea of Black-eyed Susans: plants up to three feet tall, filled with wide, three-inch yellow blossoms, with dark brown conical centers. They were a sight to behold — not ever seen before — because we always cut them down, never allowing them to reach maturity and create such a spectacle of blessing.

Do we treat our brothers and sisters in the faith like the wildflowers in my pasture; constantly running our mowers of criticism, unkind judgment, and gossip over them? Mowing them down when they need our love, encouragement, and support to mature into the people God desires them to be? We do so accidentally, sometimes unknowingly, but so often deliberately. It seems to be our nature.

Merciful God, root out the old nature in me that delights in trying to build myself up by running others down. Replace that old nature with a new one, saturated with encouragement, kindness, and patience.

EDIFY ONE ANOTHER . . . ENCOURAGE
THE FAINTHEARTED, SUPPORT THE WEAK,
BE PATIENT TOWARD ALL MEN
(1 THESSALONIANS 5:11–14).

Ten

BLOODROOT
Sanguinaria canadensis

Warmth! Loved! Protected! Those are the thoughts that flood my heart whenever I find the wildflower called Bloodroot.

Bloodroot gets its name from the red latex that fills the roots and stems. The Algonquian Indians used it for dye and ceremonial paint. The white flower, often two inches across, tops a single stem. One large, blue-green leaf seems to wrap itself gently about the lovely blossom.

In each flower, enfolded in its one leaf, I see God's love for me. Jeremiah speaks of an everlasting love; a wondrous Love that existed before time and visited earth in human form 2,000 years ago. The root of such love is the blood that Jesus shed for my sins on Calvary's cross. The power of that blood gives me access to God as Father and Friend. To think that our Lord gently wraps us in such love is to feel warm and protected, strong and empowered, humble and grateful.

Loving Jesus, I believe You love me unconditionally. I am simply wrapped in love that does not increase if I do grand and glorious service, nor does it decrease if I fail in my walk with You. I stand amazed to be enfolded in such love. I offer You praise and gratitude. Though it be in small measure, teach me to love the people in my life as You do!

HEREIN IS LOVE, NOT THAT WE
LOVED GOD, BUT THAT HE LOVED US, AND SENT
HIS SON TO BE THE PROPITIATION FOR OUR SINS
(1 JOHN 4:10).

~ Twelve ~

BLUESTAR
Amsonia tabernaemontana

No wildflower could be more appropriately named than Bluestar. The flowers are clustered about erect stems, one to three feet tall. Light blue with yellow centers, the blossoms are perfectly shaped five-pointed stars.

I came away from my first encounter with Bluestar humming bits and pieces of an old hymn: "Will There Be Any Stars In My Crown?" I could also hear my mother commenting on someone's sacrificially good deed. "They'll have stars in their crown," she would say.

Although the Bible speaks of crowns, it doesn't mention star-studded ones. But suppose my mother and the old hymn are right. Suppose the crowns awaiting us in heaven twinkle with good deeds done on earth. Suppose small deeds (even hugs and smiles) as well as sacrificial ones are embedded in the crown. What will my crown look like? How many stars will it hold? May I live so unselfishly that my crown will radiate with stars. I want it to be especially beautiful . . . I already know what I will do with such a crown.

Precious Jesus, someday I shall meet You face to face. My presence there will not be because of what I've done for You, but what You've done for me . Therefore, any crown, or reward, that I may win, I shall lovingly, gratefully, humbly, lay at Your feet.

HENCEFORTH THERE IS LAID UP FOR ME THE (VICTOR'S) CROWN OF RIGHTEOUSNESS — FOR BEING RIGHT WITH GOD AND DOING RIGHT — WHICH THE LORD, THE RIGHTEOUS JUDGE, WILL AWARD TO ME AND RECOMPENSE ME THAT (GREAT) DAY; AND NOT TO ME ONLY BUT ALSO TO ALL THOSE WHO HAVE LOVED AND YEARNED FOR AND WELCOMED HIS APPEARING (HIS RETURN)
(2 TIMOTHY 4:8; AMPLIFIED BIBLE).

Patches of bluish-purple are showing in the pasture. It is early spring and the Bluets are blooming.

Bluets are so small you need to get down on your hands and knees to see them well. Four tiny petals on a two-inch stem no bigger than my crochet thread. Only if you were really looking, would you even notice one as you walked along. However, put a bunch of Bluets together and they have the power to turn the pasture blue!

As believers in Christ, we have that power, also. Christians today are being called upon to take a stand against forces that would undermine the family and the Church. United, we have a voice that can be heard; a presence that can be seen and felt.

Bluets are also a reminder of our need of fellowship with other believers. Day-to-day living for Christ is not easy. The love and support of other Christians strengthens, inspires, and challenges our walk with God. Paul surely had this in mind when he admonished believers not to neglect the assembling of themselves together.

Holy God, thank You for the blessed fellowship of Your family, but help me to remember that the purpose of fellowship is to provide strength for service. Rouse me from my comfort zone to stand with other Christians in whatever way You direct.

I NEED YOUR HELP, FOR I WANT NOT ONLY TO SHARE MY FAITH WITH YOU, BUT TO BE ENCOURAGED BY YOURS. EACH OF US WILL BE A BLESSING TO THE OTHER (ROMANS 1:12; LIVING BIBLE).

Sixteen

CANCERWEED
Salvia lyrata

With a name like Cancerweed, this spring wildflower wins few popularity contests. Perhaps the name was appropriate long ago when the seeds were made into an ointment for open sores. Today it has a negative connotation. It is difficult to get past the "cancer" and the "weed" to truly enjoy this subdued but lovely flower. Gardeners hate weeds and we all feel a touch of fear when we hear the word cancer.

There are cancers among us equally as deadly as the physical disease:

The cancer of guilt, ceaseless gnawing within over past mistakes, never able to let past be past and live in today.

The cancer of non-acceptance, emotions ravaged with frantic efforts to change other people or circumstances.

The cancer of unforgiveness, holding onto grudges and hurts inflicted by others, allowing the hurt to fester and spread until we are destroyed.

The cancer of emptiness, forever eating away our joy, happiness, and peace. We are forever searching, never finding.

Jesus, great physician of the soul, we need healing. Heal the guilts that would destroy our serenity. Give us grace to accept what we cannot change. Supply loving strength that we may forgive those who have wronged us. And, Dear Lord, fill that awful emptiness within with Your presence.

WHEN JESUS HEARD IT HE SAITH UNTO THEM, THEY THAT ARE WELL
HAVE NO NEED OF THE PHYSICIAN, BUT THEY THAT ARE SICK.
I CAME NOT TO CALL THE RIGHTEOUS, BUT SINNERS
TO REPENTANCE (MARK 2:17).

CARDINAL FLOWER
Lobelia cardinalis

Cardinal Flowers are rare here along Second Creek. Sometimes I only see one throughout the entire season. So finding a Cardinal is a time of celebration and special joy. The one plant I found last summer blessed me with its beauty and taught a lesson as well.

As I drove across our bridge, I noticed a blotch of fiery red, about 50 feet up the creek. I stopped the car, climbed throught the barbed wire fence, and went to investigate.

There it was! A magnificent Cardinal, growing in a gravel bar, not three feet away from the edge of the creek. On occasion, after a heavy rain, our beautiful creek becomes a raging river, bringing down large trees as well as fragile flowers. Not only was the Cardinal growing in the gravel bed, poor soil conditions, but so near the creek, a perilous location. I imagine the Cardinal saying to itself, and to God, "Okay, so circumstances are far from ideal, but this is where You planted me, God. Therefore, it is here that I will bloom!"

Dear Lord, help me to follow the Cardinal's example. My circumstances may be less than perfect, but give me grace to bloom where I'm planted, too.

FOR I HAVE LEARNED HOW TO BE CONTENT
(SATISFIED TO THE POINT WHERE I AM NOT DISTURBED
OR DISQUIETED) IN WHATEVER STATE I AM
(PHILLIPPIANS 4:11; AMPLIFIED BIBLE).

COW VETCH
Vicia cracca

Without an invitation, Cow Vetch tramped into my Iris bed and proceeded to make itself at home. It ran rampant about the bed. It wrapped its tendrils tightly about the Irises. When I tried to pull it out, it simply broke off above the ground, leaving the roots to begin a second conquest of what was once a clean corner of the yard. I hated that Vetch. It was no wildflower — it was a weed! Even though the blooms were pretty, my angry eyes saw nothing but WEED, WEED, WEED!

"Look with love, hear with compassion," the Holy Spirit whispered softly. "Angry eyes will never see the lesson."

Vetches in human form marched through my mind: the domineering, overbearing kind, the troublemakers, the negative ones — impossible to please, the hateful, the selfish, the hurtful, and the cruel. Weeds to me! Wildflowers to God! I began to notice the purple patches of Cow Vetch along the highways, impressive patches. I learned that farmers often plant vetch as a cover crop; keeping the soil from eroding and later nourishing it when they plow the vetch under. It may be a "pain" to me, but in the right location and the right circumstances, vetch has beauty and usefulness.

Loving God, You love the unlovely. If I am to walk with You in obedience, I must love them, too. Help me to see past who they are, to who they can become, if transplanted into a garden of love, concern, and acceptance.

BUT I SAY UNTO YOU, LOVE YOUR ENEMIES, BLESS THEM
THAT CURSE YOU, DO GOOD TO THEM WHO DESPITEFULLY
USE YOU, AND PERSECUTE YOU
(MATTHEW 5:44).

Cross Vine gets its name from the stems; when cut diagonally, they reveal the shape of a cross. Early southeastern missionaries discovered this hidden symbol of their faith and rejoiced as they were reminded of the greatest cross of history — the center cross of Calvary.

I have never seen the vine close enough to examine leaf patterns or infant blossoms. Cross Vine's presence is revealed only by mature blossoms, fallen on the ground. It seems to delight in finding the tallest tree and then climbing to the very top.

Today, crosses are everywhere: atop church spires, on decorative jewelry, in cemeteries, even hidden in a wildflower stem. So commonplace, I wonder how many of us see them and think of the roughly-hewn wooden cross on which Jesus died. Still, we finite people need reminders, whatever their size, of the infinite. Perhaps some do see, and pause, and remember the love poured out there, His life given for ours. Remembering, we bow in gratitude and commitment, ever reaching for new heights of spiritual awareness and growth.

Loving Father, I never saw that old rugged cross on which Your Son died, but I have seen and experienced the blossoms that fell from it: forgiveness for my sins, acceptance into Your family, and the promise of eternal life. Humbly, I thank You.

BUT FAR BE IT FROM ME TO GLORY IN ANYTHING OR ANY ONE
EXCEPT IN THE CROSS OF OUR LORD JESUS CHRIST,
THE MESSIAH, THROUGH WHOM THE WORLD HAS
BEEN CRUCIFIED TO ME, AND I TO THE WORLD
(GALATIONS 6:14; AMPLIFIED BIBLE).

Twenty-four

DAYFLOWER
Commelina communis "Asiatic"

At first glance Dayflower blooms look like they have only two petals. These are large and showy and bright. Looking closer, a small white petal can be found hiding behind the pistil and stamens. Dayflowers are aptly named, as their blossoms are short-lived, they last only a single morning.

It seems sad that the uniquely lovely blossom of Dayflower lasts such a short time. But rather than feel sorrow, I rejoice that our loving God uses even this tiny creation to kindly remind me of several truths I so easily forget. In Dayflowers:

I remember that my life, however long, is also brief.

I see my need to die daily; to my selfish ambitions, to my will and wants, to hurts and anger and unforgiveness.

I choose to live in today, not allowing the past, nor the future, to destroy the beauty of NOW.

Living Lord, I have today. Tomorrow may not be mine. Slow me down. Bestow on me wisdom and determination to <u>make</u> time in this day for thoughts and acts of love toward You and others.

SO DON'T BE ANXIOUS ABOUT TOMORROW.
GOD WILL TAKE CARE OF YOUR TOMORROW
TOO. LIVE ONE DAY AT A TIME
(MATTHEW 6:34; LIVING BIBLE).

Children love Dandelions! What fun to blow the seed head, sending the tiny parachute seeds flying into the air! As children, we believed that if you made a wish and blew all the parachutes away in three blows your wish would come true. We spent countless hours wishing and blowing. I don't know that we ever got our wishes, but we never tired of the game.

Dandelions can be found from the tip of Florida to Alaska, from California to Maine. They grow from 1 to 20 inches in height, averaging six to seven inches. Around my home, Dandelions are ground huggers; one, possibly two inches tall.

Ground huggers are smart. They stay close to their source of nourishment. The wind doesn't blow them over or lawn mowers mow them down. As the ground nourishes the Dandelions, the Bible, God's love letter to us, nourishes Christians. Sometimes we wander so far away from our source of spiritual food and water that we are tossed about by winds of false teaching and untruths. We're cut down by doubt, discouragement, and complacency. We desire an easier, softer path to faith, believing anything that sounds good, looks good, or feels good as we're blown to and fro by winds of confusion.

Holy Father, Your Word is my spring of nourishment; my reservoir of faith, hope, and strength. Bind me tightly to it, and You, with cords of hunger, expectancy, and love.

THY WORD IS A LAMP UNTO MY FEET
AND A LIGHT UNTO MY PATH
(PSALM 119:105).

Twenty-eight

DEERGRASS
Rhexia virginica

The finding of Deergrass required I climb up and over an invisible wall called fear. The group of Deergrass flowers, bright pink with large yellow stamens, was easy to see. The difficulty was getting to them. We were separated by 15 feet of tall grass growing on a hillside, wet by a natural spring. The grass hissed, "Snake, snake!" The ground groaned, "Muddy, yucky!" Fear within me soothingly crooned, "Stay where you are! You can see that old flower well enough."

But Deergrass was a new flower and I couldn't see it well enough for identification. I knew the color was pink, but I was unable to tell the exact shape of the blooms or leaves. Deciding not to listen to the grass or mud, or my fear, I dashed across the 15 feet, picked a flower and dashed back again. In my hand I held a new wildflower to identify, and a symbol of victory over fear.

Life is full of patches of beautiful Deergrass separated from us by variations of unseen snakes, tall grass, and gooey mud. We can choose to stand on the sidelines and observe from a distance or we can abandon our fear and dash in — grabbing hold of life at its best and fullest. The choice is ours.

Dear God, thank You for those times I have thrown out fear and replaced it with courage. Courage to return to college at 39, and graduate three years later. Courage to learn to line dance at 58. May I never allow fear to rob me of what I want to do. You and me, together, are a team, a team that can handle anything!

FOR GOD HATH NOT GIVEN US THE SPIRIT OF FEAR, BUT OF
POWER, AND OF LOVE, AND OF A SOUND MIND
(2 TIMOTHY 1:7).

DWARF BLUE FLAG
Iris verna

Imagine my surprise the first time I happened upon a bunch of Dwarf Blue Flags. I'd always loved the wild Irises of Alaska (commonly called Flags) and now I'd found them in miniature in the south. The little 6-inch plants are so similar to the 30-inch ones of the far north. Late March sends me on a special walk, to a special place, and I find the little flags. What a delight!

Choosing a favorite wildflower would be difficult — impossible! Choosing one that simply delights me is easy; I'd pick the little Dwarf Flags. They give me an especially joyful, dance-about feeling whenever I see them. I experience that same feeling when I read in God's Word that He delights in me, in all His children. Imagine! We are a delight to God, we give Him great pleasure! Perhaps, He, too, wants to dance about when we come into His presence through prayer. He loves our fellowship. We can just pop in or meet Him at a prearranged time each day. He welcomes our visits. "Come often, My child," God assures us, "I delight in your company!"

Blessed Father, thank You for prayer, that spiritual vehicle that ushers me into Your presence. Knowing that You delight in my company encourages me to come frequently. I'm always welcomed, joyfully accepted as I am, and loved unconditionally.

HE LED ME TO A PLACE OF SAFETY,
FOR HE DELIGHTS IN ME
(PSALM 18:19; LIVING BIBLE).

FIRE PINK
Silene virginica

Fiery red color and petal tips touched by the pinking shears of God give Fire Pinks their name. They prefer wooded areas, easily seen against a background of winter browns and early spring greens. Fire Pinks are representative of a great number of wildflowers; when once established, they can be depended on to bloom in that spot year after year. I can count on finding them beneath the cedar tree, behind my compost bin and along a ten-foot section of familiar path.

Fire Pinks understand dependability. Shadrach, Meshach, and Abednego did, too. Heroes of a well-known Old Testament story, these young men would not worship the king's golden image, even though refusal meant a fiery death.

From their magnificent statement of faith and dependability come three little words of inspiration and determination — "but if not." They knew God could deliver them, but if He chose not to do so, their faith, and their faithfulness, would remain the same. If their prayers were answered, they would stand true; if their prayers were unanswered, their spiritual stance would not change. They have been an unrivaled example of dependability down through the centuries.

Unfailing Lord Jesus, as Your Father could depend on You to carry out His will, may I be dependable to carry out Yours. And if Your will leads me straight through, not around, a fiery furnace, I rest in the knowledge that You will walk through the flames with me.

OUR GOD, WHOM WE SERVE, IS ABLE TO DELIVER US FROM THE BURNING FIERY FURNACE . . . BUT IF NOT, BE IT KNOWN UNTO THEE, O KING, THAT WE WILL NOT SERVE THY GODS, NOR WORSHIP THE GOLDEN IMAGE WHICH THOU HAST SET UP (DANIEL 3:17–18).

INDIAN PINK
Spigelia marilandica

The brilliant red of Indian Pinks are easy to spot amid the green of early summer. The problem is the rarity of the species. Three summers ago I found an Indian Pink by the back gate. Last summer I discovered another behind our woodshed. In the ten years I've lived here, those are the only two Indian Pinks I've seen. Until this year, that is! There are five Indian Pinks happily growing along the path, past our swinging bridge, as it twists and turns up the hill to the mailbox.

Is it just chance that these rare flowers are growing along my well-traveled pathway? Possibly, but I prefer to think God planted them there especially for me. To quote Anatole France, "Chance is perhaps the pseudonym for God when he did not want to sign his name." As a loving Father, God delights in giving to His children. Those five Indian Pinks have been a delight for me. Growing along a path I use everyday, I've watched them grow and develop and bloom. It surely must thrill the heart of God when we, His children, choose to thank Him for the little gifts of life instead of tossing them away to "chance."

Giving Father, I believe the five Indian Pinks were planted by You, for me. I give You thanks. I also thank You for the empty parking space right in front of the store when it was raining or I was in a hurry; for the cows not getting out when I forgot to close the gate; for the moment when I happened upon a mother robin as she popped a fat worm into her baby's mouth. I choose to fill my heart with gratitude for the special gifts others call "chance."

IN EVERYTHING GIVE THANKS, FOR THIS IS THE WILL
OF GOD IN CHRIST JESUS CONCERNING YOU
(1 THESSALONIANS 5:18).

IVY LEAF
MORNING GLORY
Ipomoea Hederacea

A planted garden is a mixture of relief and joyful accomplishment. Spot of ground, divided equally into neat rows. (Well, sometimes my rows aren't so neat. The plants don't mind, they'll grow in an imperfect row.) Soon the early seeds make a line of green down the row. Sprinkled between the rows pop multitudes of various little plants — commonly called weeds!

Most of the weeds here in my Alabama garden deserve the name for the havoc they cause. However, some of these weeds are Morning Glories. Though from time to time I lose my patience with them, their beauty blesses me far beyond their nuisance ways.

One species, the Ivy Leaf Morning Glory, has taught me much about a part of life — change. The bloom of the Ivy Leaf unfolds a brilliant blue — the blue of a cloudless sky or a robin's egg. As the bloom ages, it turns purple.

I can imagine that bloom about to burst with joy over its fine blue color, basking in its own loveliness. Then — zap! It changes to purple! Life is like that. Just when I'm settled into it, all's going well, living is sky blue all the way — then zap! It changes; financial troubles, re-location, empty nest, sickness, accident, death. Life is suddenly not blue, but purple.

Change isn't comfortable, not when everything is sky blue. I resist it, fight it, yell, "Why me?" May I remember the Ivy Leaf Morning Glory in times of change. The purple blooms aren't ugly, they are every bit as beautiful as the blue ones — only different.

*Dear God, unchangeable in Your love and grace; help
me to adjust to change, knowing that in Your strength,
life can again be beautiful.*

FOR I AM THE LORD, I CHANGE NOT
(MALACHI 3:6).

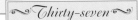

JEWELWEED
Impatiens capensis

Jewelweed is a member of a family of plants called Touch-Me-Nots. They don't have stinging hairs or thorns as the name might imply. Rather, Touch-Me-Nots get their name from their explosive fruits. The swollen seed pods burst at a touch and send their seeds flying. The blooms look like little upside-down cornucopias, reminding me to be thankful for the abundance of blessings that I enjoy.

After identifying Jewelweed and reading about its Touch-Me-Not properties, the plant brings to mind a negative lesson to shun and a possible one to copy. May I never cry out,

> Touch me not, God! I'm satisfied where I am, busy
> with my own plans, wrapped up in my own little world.
> Don't touch me with compassion for others, hunger for
> spiritual growth, or a call to deeper discipleship.
> Touch me not, God!

Instead, may my heart desire to be bursting with the fruits of the Spirit, sending them out into my world with His daily touch.

Gracious God, how thankful I am for Your touch on my life. Through prayer, Your Word, and service to others, I may also touch You. Keep my heart tender and touchable, that those whose lives meet mine may feel the jewel-like sparkle of Your love.

WHEN THE HOLY SPIRIT CONTROLS OUR LIVES HE WILL PRODUCE THIS KIND OF FRUIT IN US: LOVE, JOY, PEACE, PATIENCE, KINDNESS, GOODNESS, FAITHFULNESS, GENTLENESS, AND SELF-CONTROL (GALATIANS 5:22; LIVING BIBLE).

MAY APPLE
Podophyllum peltatum

Have you ever seen a forest floor covered with green umbrellas? That wondrous happening occurs in the spring, when the May Apples begin to grow. The plants have one or two umbrellas, or leaves. Those that have two leaves will produce one gorgeous white bloom, two inches wide, developing later into one round fruit that is edible.

It is in the one simple flower and one simple fruit of the May Apple that I have learned to let go of the past, and walk free in the present. In my teen years, I wanted so much to do grand and glorious things for God. Not only did I want to, I felt God had called me to do so. Life didn't turn out that way. I spent many years so miserable and guilt-ridden because I couldn't do the grand and glorious, that I did nothing.

Does the May Apple droop and groan because it can produce only one flower, only one fruit? No! It stands serene and declares, "I shall give to God only one flower, but it will be beautiful. My one fruit will be as sweet as honey."

Loving Father, help me to know, deep within the depths of my soul, that the simple thing, the cup of cold water, given with love in Your name, are equal with the grand and glorious in Your sight.

AND IF, AS MY REPRESENTATIVES, YOU GIVE EVEN A CUP OF COLD WATER TO A LITTLE CHILD, YOU WILL SURELY BE REWARDED (MATTHEW 10:42; LIVING BIBLE).

PEPPER ROOT
Dentaria laciniata "Toothwort"

The hillside above our swinging bridge bursts forth with life by mid-March. The wildflowers are back! It's a party; a reunion of old friends. My heart sings a greeting, "Welcome, I've been looking for you! How delightful to have you here again!"

I call each flower by name. "Hello, Anemone! Welcome Saxifrage! Trout Lily, your yellow dress is as beautiful as always. Sorrel, I've missed you. Such a dainty thing you are, Spring Beauty. Your red outfit is stunning, Fire Pink. Dwarf Flag, you are as gorgeous as ever. And . . . and. . . ."

My mind blanks! I look at the delicate wildflower with bell-shaped, pinkish-white blossoms and deeply pilated leaves. Memory fails me! It's a simple name! I know it! What is it? Only after I give up and resort to my identification books do I remember. "Of course, its name is Pepper Root!"

In John 10, Jesus portrays himself as the Good Shepherd, calling His sheep by name. He not only knows my name, He knows me: the paths I'm tempted to stray on, the greener grass that beckons me from dangerous places, the complacency of old pastures, and the fear of the rocky crags leading to new grazing grounds.

Gentle Shepherd, You know my name. You never forget it or me. Lead this sheep to pastures verdant with grasses of spiritual growth and holy intimacy.

THE GATEKEEPER OPENS THE GATE FOR HIM AND THE SHEEP HEAR HIS VOICE AND COME TO HIM, AND HE CALLS HIS OWN SHEEP BY NAME AND LEADS THEM OUT. HE WALKS AHEAD OF THEM; AND THEY FOLLOW HIM, FOR THEY RECOGNIZE HIS VOICE (JOHN 10:3–4; LIVING BIBLE).

QUEEN ANNE'S LACE
Daucus carota

Queen Anne's Lace is abundant along our country roads. It begins to bloom in early summer and seems to prefer roadsides to meadows or wooded areas.

The bloom of Queen Anne's Lace is composed of flat umbels; clusters of tiny flowers on stalks growing out from about the same point on the main stem. The flower has a distinctive identification mark, easily distinguishing it from similar plants. In the center of the group of umbels is a small, dark red flower — alike, but larger than the umbel blooms.

As the one dark bloom is the center point of Queen Anne's Lace, so Jesus desires to be the center of our lives. Those umbels represent the various areas of life: marriage, children, church, occupation, recreation, friends, goals, and ambitions. Christ calls us to put Him in the center of our lives and relationships. All of life's umbels are to radiate around Him, being influenced by His presence and will.

Jesus, You who are love in action, give me willingness to center You among the umbels of my life. And thank You, Lord, that Queen Anne's Lace loves to grow along roadsides. All summer long I am gently reminded to center myself in You.

I AM CRUCIFIED WITH CHRIST; NEVERTHELESS I LIVE; YET NOT I, BUT CHRIST LIVETH IN ME; AND THE LIFE WHICH I NOW LIVE IN THE FLESH I LIVE BY THE SON OF GOD, WHO LOVED ME AND GAVE HIMSELF FOR ME (GALATIANS 2:20).

RUELLIAS
Ruellia strepens "Wild Petunia"

I came so close to missing the lesson God had for me the day I discovered Ruellias, commonly called Wild Petunia.

There I was, right in the middle of the blackberry patch, busily picking luscious berries, dreaming of the pie I'd make for dinner. A spot of violet caught my eye. A few feet away, among the briers, grew a Wild Petunia!

Thrilled with the find of a new wildflower, as I always am, I stepped closer to examine the flower. A few moments of admiration and I returned to picking berries, dropping them, ker-plunk, ker-plunk, into my bucket. Later, carefully finding my way out of the berry patch, the Holy Spirit within me whispered, "You just saw a picture of God, don't miss it!"

In memory, I saw again the Wild Petunia, a spot of beauty, standing tall in the midst of the brier patch. Isn't that just like God? He's always there in the brier patch situations of our lives, if we will only notice. When it seems everywhere we turn, we get caught and snagged by thorns of disappointment, or sorrow, or hurt, God is there. We don't stand in that brier patch alone. His presence is there to give us comfort, hope, and strength.

Faithful God, from time to time, life may be a brier patch, but You're there with me. I thank You.

I WILL BE WITH YOU JUST AS I WAS WITH MOSES; I
WILL NOT ABANDON YOU OR FAIL TO HELP YOU
(JOSHUA 1:5; LIVING BIBLE).

SPRING BEAUTY
Claytonia virginia

I find them suddenly, unexpectedly, joyfully. After the cold and barrenness of winter, the early flowers of spring. It's an unexpected pleasure when I happen upon them. Perhaps walking across the pasture. I look down and there they are, the Spring Beauties, proclaiming glorious news. It's spring! It's spring!

The arrival of the early Spring Beauties speak in many ways of God. As we experience the seasons in our lives, we also go through seasons of the soul. All of life is not the sky blue warmth of summer. Often it is rather the gray coldness of winter. But this I know, as springs follows winter here in my Alabama home, so spring follows winter within my spirit. God is dependable. He may allow me to pass through periods of spiritual winter, trials, disappointments, sadness, and loss, but He will follow them with spring; renewal, new understanding, growth, joy, and strength.

Dependable God, help me as I go through a spiritual winter to hold on to the eternal promises of spring. I may still feel the cold air and see only barrenness, but I trust You and know that in Your dependability, I shall soon find springtime in my heart.

FOR I KNOW WHOM I HAVE BELIEVED AND AM
PERSUADED THAT HE IS ABLE TO KEEP THAT WHICH I
HAVE COMMITTED UNTO HIM AGAINST THAT DAY
(2 TIMOTHY 1:12).

TINY SPRING FLOWERS
Viola ratinesquii, Houstonia caerutea,
Claytonia virginica

God ushers in spring with a burst of the tiniest of flowers. Bluets, Spring Beauties, Wild Pansy, and numerous others are wondrously lovely, but they will be seen by only a few people. They're simply too small to be noticed as most folks roller coaster through their busy lives.

So . . . I wonder. Why did God bother? Why not plant roses, mums, dahlias, and sunflowers? Big! Bright! Showy! Keep the flowers large enough for us to enjoy them as we zip by, hurrying from one place to another.

Tiny wildflowers dance to a joyful tune, for those who will stop and listen and see. They sway, bend, and bow, declaring:

> **Small things are important.**
> **God cares about the minute matters of our lives.**
> **No circumstance is too trivial to talk over with God.**
> **Each day, enjoy the small acts in this drama of life.**
> **Be thankful for tiny things.**
> **Great blessings come in undersized packages.**

Wondrous God, when I pace my days to see and hear and touch the smallest things in my world, I am blessed with joyous anticipation, peace beyond understanding, and strength for the boulders when they rumble my way.

LET HIM HAVE ALL YOUR CARES AND WORRIES, FOR HE IS ALWAYS THINKING ABOUT YOU AND WATCHING EVERYTHING THAT CONCERNS YOU (1 PETER 5:7; LIVING BIBLE).

TOADSHADE
Trillium sessile

Toadshade belongs to the Trillium family of wildflowers. The name Trillium comes from the Latin for "three." Toadshade, as do all Trilliums, has three leaves, three green sepals, three colored petals, and (surrounded by six stamens) a three-chambered pistil topped by three spreading stigmas.

The great doctrine of the Trinity is easily represented in Toadshade; three in one; God — Father, Son, Holy Spirit. I understand the Trinity simply, as a child. I accept it in childlike faith. God, the Father, loves me (John 3:16). God the Son died for me and now lives to intercede for me (Hebrews 7:25). God the Holy Spirit dwells within me as comforter and teacher (John 14: 16, 26).

Dear God, Holy Father, Lord Jesus, Blessed Spirit –
You give meaning and purpose to my life. Create within me an
insatiable desire to know You better. Help me to cultivate my relation-
ship with You, giving it that essential element so hard to come
by – time! I am often so busy with "good" choices that
I have little time left for the best.

FOR MY DETERMINED PURPOSE IS THAT I MAY KNOW HIM —
THAT I MAY PROGRESSIVELY BECOME MORE DEEPLY AND
INTIMATELY ACQUAINTED WITH HIM, PERCEIVING AND
RECOGNIZING AND UNDERSTANDING THE WONDERS OF
IIIS PERSON MORE STRONGLY AND MORE CLEARLY
(PHILIPPIANS 3:10; AMPLIFIED BIBLE).

In early March I walk a familiar path up a certain hill and delight to find the Trout Lilies. They get their name from the brownish-green mottling of their leaves; coloring similar to the trout swimming in the nearby creek.

The hillside is covered with individual leathery leaves poking out of the ground. The one-leaf plants are first-year plants and do not bloom. The mature plants are two years old, have two leaves, and produce the bright yellow blossom, one of spring's loveliest.

Trout Lilies remind me that I am on a spiritual journey; I have not arrived at my destination. Often I feel the slowness, the shallowness of my depth of maturity, producing few spiritual blooms of blessing. I try to be patient with myself, remembering that I am changing, however slowly, into His likeness.

Trout Lilies also challenge me to look into a spiritual mirror from time to time. As a Christian, I am named for Jesus Christ. Do I look like Him in thought and action? Do folks look at me and think of Him?

Patient Father, I am so impatient with myself. Encourage me to accept me as I am, because You do. Give me willingness to discipline myself in ways that will produce growth. When I fail, grant me grace to ask Your forgiveness. Pick me up, dust me off, and strengthen me to press on!

I DON'T MEAN TO SAY I AM PERFECT. I HAVEN'T LEARNED ALL I SHOULD EVEN YET, BUT I KEEP WORKING TOWARD THAT DAY WHEN I WILL FINALLY BE ALL THAT CHRIST SAVED ME FOR AND WANTS ME TO BE (PHILLIPPIANS 3:12; LIVING BIBLE).

TRUMPET CREEPER
Campsis radicans

When the July sun sends me scurrying for my shady backyard swing or a late afternoon swim in the creek, it's time to look for Trumpet Creeper. Overgrown fence rows, neglected by their owners, are favorite locations for this climber. Its blazing cluster of trumpet-shaped flowers, ranging from orange to scarlet, are easy to spot.

A musical note of excitement stirs within me and rises to a crescendo of praise! Trumpet Creeper portrays the second coming of Jesus Christ. I imagine Him and His Father, God, conversing on that morning of all mornings. His Father says;

Today is the day, My Son! All is ready! Sound the trumpets! Break open the sky! Go! Bring my children home!

My heart acts out the drama. I hear the trumpets! I look up and see my Lord in the clouds! I wait patiently as the believing dead of all ages rise to meet Him and then wonder of all wonders, I, too, begin my glorious ascent to Jesus.

Living Lord, my ears are listening. My luggage is packed with all I need — Your love and amazing grace. My ticket is stamped "Paid In Full At Calvary." Come, Lord Jesus! I'm ready!

FOR THE LORD HIMSELF WILL COME DOWN FROM HEAVEN WITH A MIGHTY SHOUT . . . AND THE GREAT TRUMPET-CALL OF GOD. BELIEVERS WHO ARE DEAD WILL BE FIRST TO RISE TO MEET THE LORD. THEN WE WHO ARE ALIVE WILL BE CAUGHT UP WITH THEM IN THE CLOUDS TO MEET THE LORD IN THE AIR AND REMAIN WITH HIM FOREVER (1 THESSALONIANS 4:16–17; LIVING BIBLE).

VIOLETS
Viola pedata, Viola sororia,
Viola pubescens, Viola sagittata

I've read that there are more than 60 species of violets in North America, more than 500 species worldwide. All violets have five petals; the lower petal somewhat larger with lines leading to the nectar-laden center flower.

Around my rural home, I have found four kinds. Downy Yellows sport their heart-shaped leaves. Another heart-shaped leafer, the Common Blue, produces blossoms ranging from purple to lavender to white. Purple Arrow Leaf has leaves shaped like arrowheads. Bird's Foot violets (known locally as Blue Roosters) have deeply cut, lacy leaves. The blossom may be completely violet or the top two petals may be a deep bluish-purple. Whatever their color, or shape of their leaves, they're all violets. They all belong to the same family.

I've never heard one violet criticize another because it is different. Nor have I seen one puffed up with pride because it is "better than you-know-who!" Let's learn a lesson from the violets. Whatever our "species," Methodist, Baptist, Presbyterian, Catholic, Pentecostal, non-denominational, we are all Christians. God is our Father, Jesus our Saviour and friend, the Holy Spirit our comforter and guide. Our given names differ, but we have the same surname: Christian! We are part of the family of God!

Dear Heavenly Father, It must break Your heart when we believers, Your children, fuss and fight! Forgive us. Grant us grace that we may minimize our differences and maximize our likenesses. As brothers and sisters in Christ, help us to resemble one another in love, compassion, and joy.

❧

AND NOW THIS WORD TO ALL OF YOU: YOU SHOULD BE LIKE ONE
BIG HAPPY FAMILY, FULL OF SYMPATHY TOWARD EACH OTHER,
LOVING ONE ANOTHER WITH TENDER HEARTS AND HUMBLE MINDS
(1 PETER 3:8; LIVING BIBLE).

VIRGINIA BLUEBELLS
Mertensia virginica

Babies! Virginia Bluebells remind me of babies. Not for their height; at upwards of two and one-half feet, they are unusually tall for early spring flowers. Not for their large, oval leaves nor the bell-shape of their blossoms. Colors: it is their colors that are reminiscent of babies. The buds are the daintiest pink, the flowers a perfect baby blue.

The writer of Hebrews admonishes Christians to desire the milk of God's Word as a new baby nurses at its mother's breast. Contented and warm with the closeness of her presence, infant and mother together enjoy a sweet fellowship. Nourished by its mother, the baby will advance to solid food, grow to adulthood and request steak and potatoes instead of milk. Everyone rejoices.

Sadly, many in God's family never grow up. As spiritual infants, they go through life nourished only by a few drops of milk on Sunday morning. They don't even nurse. They're spoon-fed. They never snuggle up to God's Word, nursing for themselves the truths that lead to maturity. Only skimming the surface of Scripture, they never experience its deeper truths. Always babies, not ever spiritual adults, they are unable to provide nourishment to young ones in the faith.

Beloved Holy Spirit, I desire to grow up. Create in me a hunger that will not be satisfied with baby bottles. I crave spiritual food dug deep from within the garden of Your Word.

YOU HAVE BEEN CHRISTIANS A LONG TIME NOW, AND YOU OUGHT TO BE TEACHING OTHERS, BUT INSTEAD YOU HAVE DROPPED BACK TO THE PLACE WHERE YOU NEED SOMEONE TO TEACH YOU ALL OVER AGAIN THE VERY FIRST PRINCIPLES IN GOD'S WORD. YOU ARE LIKE BABIES WHO CAN DRINK ONLY MILK, NOT OLD ENOUGH FOR SOLID FOOD (HEBREWS 5:12; LIVING BIBLE).

WAPATO
Sagittaria latifolia

It was well into fall, most of the trees had changed their summer dresses of green to yellow and red and orange. A sadness settled over me. The wildflowers were gone. Winter lurked around the corner. I stopped looking for flowers, confident I had seen all there was to see, to discover. A week or so later I happened upon Wapato!

A member of the Arrowhead family, Wapato was easy to identify: arrowhead-shaped leaves, three-petaled white flowers, perfect ball-shaped fruits, growing in water.

My "end of the season" discovery has taught me a valuable lesson concerning the hidden treasures of God. Never underestimate the power of His Word nor the adventure of walking with Him. When I think I know a particular passage of Scripture backward and forward, inside and out, the Holy Spirit brings a new truth to light. When I think I understand all about His will for me, the fellowship we share, or His working to root out the ugliness in me, He reveals anew himself and our special friendship.

Dearest Friend, the privilege of personally knowing You is the treasure of my life. I cherish the years we've shared together. A friendship like ours is never stagnant. It is forever new, moving, growing. Praise be Your name, there's more . . . there's more . . . there's more!

CALL TO ME AND I WILL ANSWER YOU AND SHOW YOU GREAT
AND MIGHTY THINGS, FENCED IN AND HIDDEN, WHICH
YOU DO NOT KNOW   DO NOT DISTINGUISH AND
RECOGNIZE, HAVE KNOWLEDGE OF AND UNDERSTAND
(JEREMIAH 33:3; AMPLIFIED BIBLE).

WILD PINK ROSES
Rosa setigera, Rosa acicularis

When I hear the word "rose," I mentally picture the gorgeous bloom of the two bushes alongside my house or a fragrant Valentine bouquet. God's great flower garden contains roses, too. The leaves of all wild pink roses are much the same as domesticated roses, but the blooms are much simpler, containing only five pink petals.

I have observed these roses in forested areas near my home in Alabama, also in northern Canada and Alaska. Although they look alike, what a difference there is in size and abundance. Prairie Roses in Alabama hardly qualify to be called bushes; they are spindly, fragile-looking plants. In Alaska, they're strong vigorous bushes covering huge areas, laden with blooms. After the petals fall away, the red hips (seedpods, valued for the high vitamin C content) grow large and are gathered for making rose hip jelly or drying into "raisins."

What makes the difference? Is it simply species? I suspect it is climate. Long, hot, lazy days of southern summers versus long, cold, dark nights of northern winters. The roses seem to thrive where it is harsh, difficult, and challenging.

We Christians can learn from the wild rose. Lives of ease, which we think we'd prefer, leave us weak and unproductive. Lives that must daily battle trying circumstances, mountainous problems, and wearisome people, produce strong, vigorous, beautiful testimony to God's faithfulness and provision.

Wise Father, banish my desires for lazy days of ease. Challenge me to accept the difficult situations in my life, knowing that it is in the hard times that I will grow strong and produce the most blooms for Your glory.

AND AFTER YOU HAVE SUFFERED A LITTLE WHILE, THE GOD OF ALL GRACE — WHO IMPARTS ALL BLESSINGS AND FAVOR — WHO HAS CALLED YOU TO HIS OWN ETERNAL GLORY IN CHRIST JESUS, WILL HIMSELF COMPLETE AND MAKE YOU WHAT YOU OUGHT TO BE, ESTABLISH AND GROUND YOU SECURELY, AND STRENGTHEN AND SETTLE YOU (1 PETER 5:10; AMPLIFIED BIBLE).

"Share the Faith Flower" would be a most fitting name for Yellow Wood Sorrel. The greatest joy of any Christian is to impart their faith to someone else. The Sorrels portray wise tips for sharing.

Seed pods of Yellow Wood Sorrel stand upright like little candles on a candlestick. In the fifth chapter of Matthew, Jesus describes us, His followers, as lights. He doesn't say we should be; He says we are. Is my light bright enough to light the pathway of faith for someone else to follow? Do I block its warm glow with unkind words, thoughts, or actions?

The leaves of all sorrels are made of three heart-shaped leaflets. Hearts speak of love. If we share our faith from a loveless heart, our words are just so much "sounding brass or tinkling symbol" (1 Corinthians 13:1).

The stems and leaves of all Wood Sorrels have a sour taste that adds a "zing" to a salad. However, eating too much oxalic acid, the chemical causing the sourness, tends to inhibit the absorption of calcium in the body. Let's not be too "pushy" with our witness for Christ. Gently, lovingly, let us sprinkle our conversation so others will taste and see how good He is. Seek the leading of the Lord for the words to speak and when to say them. Too many words, spoken too strongly in inappropriate circumstances, can block the ability of the heart to absorb what is said.

Lord Jesus, I love You. I desire to share with others what You have done for me. The salad I pass around to them is simply the strength and hope I have found in You. Help me to sprinkle it with tender love, sweet concern, and delicious joy.

BUT IN YOUR HEARTS SET CHRIST APART HOLY (AND ACKNOWLEDGE HIM) AS LORD. ALWAYS BE READY TO GIVE A LOGICAL DEFENSE TO ANYONE WHO ASKS YOU TO ACCOUNT FOR THE HOPE THAT IS IN YOU, BUT DO IT COURTEOUSLY AND RESPECTFULLY (1 PETER 3:15; AMPLIFIED BIBLE).

MELVA STEPHENS LARD

worked for several years in the education field
before retiring with her husband to their
Alabama farm. She has been a student of
wildflowers for quite some time.
This is her first book.

STEVE McGUIRE

is a much-in-demand artist in the Ozarks of
southern Missouri and northern Arkansas.
He lives with his family in
Springfield, Missouri.